Getting Unstuck

A fresh look at business practices

Cindy Pate and Shawn Pate

ISBN: 978-0-473-48062-2 (softcover)
ISBN: 978-0-473-48063-9 (kindle)
ISBN: 978-0-473-48064-6 (pdf)

DEDICATION

To the friends and family members who have helped us along the way.
I thank you for being the support we needed.
To our boys, may your path always be filled with love and adventure. Thank you
for being part of this crazy journey of entrepreneurship.

This book serves as a reminder that no matter where life takes you, never give up
on your dreams.

CONTENTS

ACKNOWLEDGMENTS

There are many people who have helped us and who we have learnt from over the years and each one sharing a part of their knowledge with us. This book is in honor of the trailblazers before us.

The road to be an entrepreneur is not an easy one but one that has so many blessings along the way. I want to take this time to acknowledge all the entrepreneurs and business owners out there who have taken on that challenge and decided to make a difference.

I want to say a special thanks to Rowena, for taking on babysitter duties while we tackled the world of business. Without her help this book would still just be an idea.

1 INTRODUCTION

I walked in to drop my boys off at kindy, as I usually did, and this time I decided to have a chat at reception. One of the staff members was telling me how tired she was, and I was saying, "yeah, I hear you. I can't keep my eyes open". What came next shocked me.

She very quickly replied with "how can you be tired you do nothing all day and get to relax"

This is the moment I realised that to the outside world, my life seemed idyllic. My boys don't have to go to kindy, that is why half the time they come in an hour later than their scheduled start. They go to kindy to have a break from their parent and have more kid time.

On the outside it looks like we have this perfect lifestyle and yes we currently do, and I would not have it any other way , however that was not always the case.

It reminds me of a time when I was at the mall walking around and window shopping. You know those moments where you look at clothes through the window and imagine yourself one day owning it. When you play that familiar sounding track of "One day the tide will turn and things will come right". But for now you have to make do with the same outfits you have owned for the last 5 years. Yes I used to do that every so often, it kept me focussed on things that I wanted in life, not just material but it gave me a better grasp on reality. It kept me focussed on the goal. I even once dressed up real nice and went into a Louis Vuitton store and felt what it would feel like to not have someone question if you can afford an item.

During that time every cent we had was used to cover debt or food. There was no money to just do as we please. It was tight.

It is so funny because Shawn and I joke about it a lot now, on how we were so poor that we had to eat seafood for dinner. But there was a stage where we would eat just prawns and potatoes for dinner.

Now prawns sounds like such a luxury item but it was far from it. At the time it was cheaper per kilogram to buy prawns than it was to buy items like chicken, let alone steak, and you can use less prawn. It was not even an option for us to look at chicken, those were considered a treat and something we shared between us. So when family invited us over for any occasion we made sure it would be around a meal so we could get a good meal in.

So now, as you can imagine, when someone gets jealous at the life I currently live or the food I may or may not be buying I just smile because I know that I worked my butt off to get it and I could not be prouder.

You see Shawn and I noticed something when it comes to people wanting to have a business or financial freedom. So many people say they want it, but they are so stuck in this bubble of, work work work and then moan about having to work and then repeating the cycle all over again. Or you get some who have left their traditional job to go at it alone but have no real idea what they are doing and have become stuck, only making just enough sales to sustain themselves but no growth. Having no clue what they are doing and each month they are following the next shiny object. I have seen many people go down this road of thinking "this is the one to make me rich" and it never is for them. Sometimes it has nothing to do with the product, it has to do with them always being in scramble mode, never fully getting the grasp of something before moving on.

It seems to be this continual cycle of getting stuck and not being able to get out of the hamster wheel and truly focus on what is going on and what the problem is.

You see the problem most people face when trying to break the cycle is that they decide to do it and that is where it ends. It is like the new year's resolution that gets made but never followed through with. "This year I will run more, or eat better". There is no real commitment just idle words that sound good to say in a conversation.

In order to break the cycle completely you need to Decide, Commit, Do. That means you do not do anything in half measures, if you decide that you can no longer do this 9-5 gig and you need to change

then decide to do it, commit to what your action plan is, and do it. It

is not the easiest thing to do but until you fully commit and do it,

you will always stay stuck living your life, on the fence, and not giving

it your all.

Nothing will change or even begin to change until you decide to

break the cycle of just saying idle words and actually commit to the

words you have just spoken. If you say you are going to run more,

then make a firm commitment, put on your shoes and get running.

The shoes are not going to do it alone.

We live the Decide, Commit, Do philosophy and because of it we

have had so many opportunities come our way and could not be

more grateful. When you take deliberate action things start changing.

Living life in half measures means nothing gets done or achieved.

Your life always seems to be in this loop of wanting more and never

achieving it. It is through taking action that brought us to writing this

book. This book is all about helping you get unstuck and gives a

fresher look at business practices. Not only that but it starts showing you what is possible in life when you truly commit to the words you speak and take action.

The beauty of the two of us working together is that we are so different and that brings more than one viewpoint and idea to the table, which means that we can get a different perspective on things. For most small businesses this is not the case and not everyone is able to employ someone like us to come in and give you a fresher perceptive and coach and mentor you. So Getting UnStuck is our solution to that problem. You will see what we did and how we tackle the start to finish of a new venture or one that is just in its infancy. You have the chance to see things from another set of eyes and hopefully open your eyes up to new possibilities and ideas.

It is a chance to get a glimpse over our shoulder and see what we did in the beginning, how we got our start in the online world of business.

So with that, enjoy the book. Take your time with it, but not too much time. It's intentionally compact, and has been developed in such a way that, if complete immersion is you thing, you can smash through it in a weekend.

I will suggest marking it up because not only is it a book, it is a working guide.

We are not holding anything back so you will get what we did and at the end of it have an action plan to help you succeed.

Now before you go and flip through the pages and skip through the material and cherry pick what you want to read. I urge you to stop and do this the right way. There is a process to follow and in order for you to get the most out of this you need to do it the right way. Start at the beginning and take the journey with us, then go back and re-read your highlights.

2 JOURNEY

We are all on a path of discovery.

In order to get anything, or in order to achieve any real success in life, we need to acknowledge the journey that we are on. It may not be on the path we thought we would be on, but we are certainly on a journey.

If you had to talk to me when I was a little girl and tell me that I would be an entrepreneur, I would have looked at you sideways. The way I grew up, the word entrepreneur was not even in our vocabulary. The closest we got was business owners. Which was referred to as a "one man band operation" because it was essentially that, someone who decided to buy themselves a job and call it a business. That seems to be what a lot of people are still doing in this day and age. Buying themselves a job because they can't fit into the current "work model". And it is really sad to see because it comes with more stress than just working for someone else, but not much more reward.

Shawn, on the other hand, grew up in an a business environment. So for him it was not too much of a stretch to where he ended up, because he essentially just carried on doing what they had always done. To him business was what put food on the table, and in my case working for someone else is what put food on the table.

As you can see we both came from very different backgrounds but find ourselves on the same path and journey right now.

The thing is, where you started in life plays an impact on where you are now but it does not and should never define who you are now.

Your environment and history play a small part in your journey. The biggest factor is you and your drive to change it.

I can run off countless names of people who were once in a terrible situation and turned it all around, and the reverse is also true. There are many people who grew up like Shawn did but instead of building on that legacy ended up having nothing at all, and end up stuck scrambling for money each month.

The reason some succeed where others fail is due to one thing and one thing only - mindset. Your thoughts and actions affect the situation you are in and the journey you are on.

This is not some new age jargon or some flimsy concept, this is what actually makes all the difference.

Do you think companies like Apple and Microsoft would be around if their founders did not have a strong belief and mindset. The answer is No. They believed that they could create something and they went out and did it. They did not let their environment stop them from growing.

You see, right now, at this very moment, you have to choose to either build a business or do a 9-5 job. You need to make a choice on which journey you want to be on. Each one comes with their own risks and rewards but you have to choose. If you think you can do both, you will probably stay stuck, and this we learnt the hard way. If you try and work full time and do something on the side, it will always be a hobby that may eventually replace the income from your 9-5 but that is about it. You will be buying yourself a job. And to be honest it really is not worth the stress because guess what, you can't have any sick days because the buck stops with you.

It feels nice to say you have your own business but nice feelings don't pay the bills, nor does stress.

This book is about taking you on the journey of discovering who you are and what business you want and how you can grow it to have a team and make a real impact.

Now before we do anything else I want to ask you a few questions, take some time and put the book down to answer this one.

Why do you want a business, or if you have one already, why?

Why do you want to be an entrepreneur?

Why have you chosen this journey?

What drives you to want this?

It may not be something that you fully thought about but, what is your why? For each one of us it is different but I want you to start thinking about your why.

2 BELIEF

"Belief is a beautiful armour

But makes for the heaviest sword" *John Mayer*

I'm sure we've all heard some version of the saying "you must believe to achieve" so many times that it's become something we don't even take any notice of. It starts to sound like a parent telling their child to clean their room, you hear the words but don't take notice.

In order for you to get the most out of your business and have success, you need to have a strong belief. I'm not talking about a specific religious belief here, I'm talking about knowing that you can achieve your goals. Not guessing or assuming, but knowing. This is the reason that athletes spend so much time practicing, so that when it comes to crunch-time they don't need to guess because they know they can. Without belief you are setting yourself up for failure. To achieve anything you need to believe that you can achieve it.

I grew up in a family business, that my parents had started when I was only 2 years old. So business was all I knew, lived and breathed. I saw deals being made, contracts negotiated, and enjoying the lifestyle it brought us. Negotiations where how I lived my life. I even negotiated what I got in my school lunchbox. I will never forget the first time I flew first class as a kid. At that time I was 10 and felt like king of the world, with no idea that in a few short years my life would change dramatically.

I was in my first year of university when something happened that rocked my world beyond imagination. A moment that I did not realise at the time would affect me for years to come.

While I was just starting a law degree the tax office decided to 'investigate' our family business. What this means is that a team of people in dark suits come in and take all your files and freeze all your accounts for as long as the investigation takes. Now as you can imagine, I had no idea what was going on and came home to what felt like death. The offices were empty and there was sheer panic. We couldn't work, clients couldn't be invoiced, we had no idea who owed us money, no staff could get paid and no suppliers could get paid. We had no means to even buy food.

This must be what hell feels like, and we were certainly living it. I tried to bravely hold things together with words like "we've got this", "they can't keep us down" and "we'll be back", but inside I didn't believe it. Inside we were all dying.

With pretty much just the clothes on our back and what we could carry we were forced to leave the family home.

I rebuilt a life as best as I could, and at the age of 24 had placed myself in some amazing opportunities like being able to work with famous names and contracting at cabinet ministerial level. I managed to build up a businesses in a short space of time that made big waves and got noticed. And you know what? They ended up failing. They reached a certain high and failed, one after another I had business do the same. I stopped counting after the 11th business died in flames.

It felt like no matter what I did, I couldn't catch a break, and then it hit me. I had to get my head in the game. If you're interviewing prospective tenants, and get to hear about how terrible every previous landlord was, then the problem is probably with the tenant's attitude. The same applies to business. If you keep being dealt with the same bad hand, then the problem is probably you. There's no way that the whole world could conspire against you.

You see my belief around business was still set to the belief that if you build something worth taking, then at some point someone will come along and take it away. This was the take-away from the most traumatic event in my life and even if not completely logical it formed a subconscious block and a self-fulfilling prophesy.

It was not until I started believing in myself, focussed on my mindset and tackled my fears that I succeeded. Holding on to your fears will keep you down. It will ensure that you never reach your full potential. Fear really is the illusion we place on our self and we hold on to it so much that we start self-sabotaging, which in turn reinforces the fear. It is a vicious cycle to be in.

I am now a father, husband and business mentor and I would have had none of that if I continued to let fear control my life and define me. Fear is an amazing motivator, but a cruel and relentless master. So let's take some action, get unstuck and Decide, Commit , Do.

What I want you to do now is to own up to your fears. In order for you to achieve your goals you need to first acknowledge your fears.

So let's do just that. It is not easy admitting you have fears, but let's be honest and real for a bit here. I still, every now and then, have those fears creep in, but over time it gets easier to recognise the self-doubt and push it aside. Admitting you have a fear does not make you less of a person, we are all human. What really holds you back is elevating that fear and empowering it by maintaining it at an emotional level.

I have a little exercise I want you to try, it's a way of taking control back and getting you unstuck.

So grab a piece of paper and lets do its.

Take some time and write three to five root fears down, the main aim is to get something down on paper. It doesn't matter if you think it's silly, this if for your eyes only. The aim is to get you thinking about them.

I've included an example to get you going.

Example Fear

> # I am scared that I will not have a successful business.

I know it can be hard to put those fears down to papers and actually acknowledge them. But trust me it will help you in the long run to get it all out.

Take some time and look at the fears that you just jotted down and now start to think about why you have those fears. What makes you think that way. The aim is to shift control of the emotion behind the fear from our subconscious to our conscious mind where we can harness it. The first step is to acknowledge the fear and emotion it triggers.

For each one of us something in our past caused that fear. Whether it was something that happened to us or something we witness. It all stems from an event - a lesson we picked up along the way.

For Cindy, one of her beliefs was that in order to have money you have to work three jobs because that was the example she knew, so why would one business solve that problem. An event / lesson learnt in the past affects how you see things in the future and affects how you tackle them.

In order to now tackle your fears, we need to break them and change the thought pattern. The way we do that is to look at each fear you jotted down and give it a new narrative, something that you can look at when you feel the same negative emotions creeping in.

You need a conscious process to shift control from a subconscious reaction to an active reinforcement. This is a long and constant process because our subconscious minds are so much more powerful and faster than our conscious minds, but they're still programmable.

So let's looks at that example from before and at how we can change that situation.

Break the Fear

I will

succeed

if I keep

going.

Take your fear and look at something positive, it helps to think: what advice you would give your children, family member or close friend. A lot of the time the advice we need to hear or lessons we need to learn is what we teach and tell others around us. Sometimes we need to practice what we preach.

Let's start BUILDING YOUR BELIEF,

Belief is what makes us who we are. What we believe in is what dictates what we do and how we do it. It forms the core of our being. Some of us have our beliefs based on religious practices, others on lessons we were taught as kids. No matter how they are formed it is what dictates our actions.

So it makes sense that when it comes to business we have beliefs around it as well. Some of what you may believe will be tied to the fears we just looked at. So in order to get you starting this journey on the right footing, we need to make sure we set up a new core belief around your business.

Right now you have the ability to achieve great things and the only thing stopping you is your own self-doubt, and the limiting belief you have set for yourself.

Sure, roadblocks do pop up, but you have not failed until you stop trying, and it's only your belief and mindset that will fuel you and make sure you keep coming back.

What I want you to do is start thinking about the reasons you will succeed, why you are doing this and what it will mean to truly nail this. It is like creating a vision board around your business. To get you started we have created some words to guide you in this process.

Take some time and fill in the blanks on the next page.

Really think about it. I cannot answer this for you, so this is where some soul searching is needed. Take as much time as you need, but find the answers from within.

These may be difficult questions to answer, but if you approach this exercise honestly and sincerely, the new realisations that they open will make a profound difference to your business life. Whenever you get stuck, you can go back to this moment and look at what you wrote and remind yourself why you are capable of success.

Building your belief

> I am capable of
> succeeding because.......

> When I feel
> stuck I will.......

> When doubt creeps in I
> will remember that.......

The belief you are creating here is your go-to. When you feel stuck or not sure why you are even on this journey, I want you to look at what you wrote down.

Feel free to add to the list, remember to keep it positive as this is what will keep you on track and make you see and realise that you've got this.

3 WHAT MARKET ARE YOU IN?

What is your business?

What do you do?

Now let's get into discussing your business and putting all the pieces of the puzzle together.

So what is your business ?

This is a question that may seem fairly simple, but believe me, so many overlook this and get it wrong. It is not as simple as just saying, I am a hairdresser, for example. When it comes to what your business is, we need to look at defining and refining it.

You need to define exactly what your actual business is. Are you a service based, product based, or info product based business? The easiest way to define this answer, is to look at what you are actually being paid or going to be paid to do. So if you are a hairdresser, for example, then you are in the service industry. Which is trading time for money.

If your business is not that clear cut, you can define it by finding out from your customers why they came to you and not a competitor. Why are they giving you their money? Is it for the service they are getting, the products you have or the information you share.

A few years ago, I had a photography studio specialising in new-born babies, and honestly it was more a like a spa for babies. There were nice comfy couches, the room was always warm with soothing music just drifting you to sleep. I had many a mommy fall asleep while I was photographing her baby because the setting was just so warm, safe and relaxing. The service even included some pampering for the new mom. Just thinking about it puts me in a relaxing calm mood.

The problem was that in my studio I was getting a mixed bag of clients, some were my ideal client and others where not. The 'nots' caused me stress and made me doubt the value of my work and therefore my value. They just wanted digital images at the cheapest possible price. They saw no value in my art and had no appreciation for the time and skill it takes to present the portraits that I proudly offered. For a long time I could not understand what I was doing wrong, and trying to keep the wrong clients happy was emotionally taxing.

What I realised was that my ideal client wanted the full experience and to be taken on a journey while capturing a priceless moment. They understood that this was a moment they could never get back again, and that every part of this journey was special and to be cherished. The other clients who I had booking my services just wanted digital images for social media.

It took me a while to realise what I was doing wrong in the studio. I was sending out mixed messages. What was my studio actually? Was it about capturing a moment or was it just a shoot and burn studio? One is a service, and the other a product. As an artist I never saw my work as a product, but in trying to compete in the marketplace, this is how most of my market saw me. Each one of these played to a different demographic, and until I realised this I was the owner of a business that I was not entirely happy with. To be honest I had a business that I started regretting having, and it became a chore to be part of it each day. All because I was not working with the clients I wanted and needed.

All I wanted was my ideal clients, but I had no idea that I was the reason that I was not getting only those ideal clients through the door consistently. What I got instead was the need to constantly defend myself, hearing things like "but my phone takes fantastic pictures", which is why I felt forced to compete on price, to sell a product.

I need you to take an honest look at your business now, or the business you imagine creating, and see what your business is. Don't do what I did and just accept any sale, really define what type of business you are in. I was calling myself both service and product when honestly I was a service-based business. The product was just a physical representation of my service. When moms came to me, it was because they had been told about the fantastic service, and that they could relax for a few hours after the ordeal of labour - this is what my ideal clients told me when I asked.

So if you currently have a few clients, I urge you to ask them why they are your clients. If you are just starting out then that is fine as well, because you have a clean slate and can make sure you define yourself from the start.

Do this exercise now and then get back to reading the book. Seriously – put it down and spend some time figuring this out. Write it down somewhere. But stop reading and do this now.

The book will be here when you get back.

Now that you have a better understanding of, and have defined what business you are in, we can dive deeper and define your market and let you in on a secret we learnt.

There are usually only three core human needs that we market to when it comes to marketing in business. I like to call them the Golden 3.

The Golden 3 is something Shawn and I had to learn the hard way. After years of trying to figure things out for ourselves we finally stumbled onto this nugget of wisdom on a Russel Brunson webinar, and I honestly wish we had known them sooner.

The reason for that is because once you understand the Golden 3 markets everything else becomes easier in marketing your business. What you offer your clients or your sales message needs to speak to one of the three.

1. Health

So the first one is Health, are you selling something that will target that market? That market is wellbeing, fitness, food, spirituality, wholeness, anything to do with being healthy. The health market is pretty self-explanatory.

2. Wealth

Next we have Wealth. Does what you sell target the wealth market? So, that is anything that has to do with finances, increasing an asset of some sort, investing, business, abundance. You get where I am going with this one. As an example, even though it has a massive focus on mindset and personal development, this book would fall into the wealth market.

3. Relationship

The final market is Relationship, and this market is one that can sometimes trip people up. Relationship can be of an intimate nature, or family, it can even involve building a team. It has to do with forming a connection or a bound. A good example to showcase this is razor blades, those commercials showing a nicely shaven man and a women looking at him. That is not showing health, or wealth - even though he may be in a suit. It is showing relationship. The ad is showing the guy that: if you use this razor, women will look at you -

and if you want the girl, use the razor.

Take my studio, at the beginning I was not even looking at the

Golden 3 markets and I was just all over the show with my

advertising. Once I figured out that I was a service business catering

to the Relationship market there was nothing stopping me. I was

then able to focus and was getting consistent clicks on my ads, and

from the right people.

No matter what it is you do or sell, it will always come back to one of

the Golden 3. It will not steer you wrong. As long as your sales

message speaks to one of the 3, you will find less confusion in your

audience and confusion is what kills sales.

The reason I share the Golden 3 needs with you so early on in this

book, and not later, is to start giving you a clear direction of what

business you are in. There is no point in going through this process,

only to find out that you are targeting the wrong market, and your

entire plan must change.

The Golden 3 only applies when it comes to marketing your business and getting your presence known in the market place. So if we go back to the hairdresser example. The business the hairdresser is in, is a service based one with their marketing being targeted at the need for relationship. Clients choose to go to a hairdresser to make themselves feel good and thereby be more confident and attractive to their desired mate.

4 COMPETITION

Competition is good.

Embrace it.

Learn from it.

Grow with it.

Looking at your competition every few months is a good way to get back in touch with your market and see what new is happening. So let's look at them.

First, don't be scared by this, the aim is for you to get a better understanding of what others are doing as compared to yourself.

I have spoken to a lot of business owners who are not comfortable doing this.

Remember we are just researching who they are and what they are doing. All we are doing is window shopping. Do not do anything unethical here. Remember window shopping is just looking.

Your competitors may not always be obvious, but they are there. Any option that will cause clients to take their money elsewhere is a competitor. If you sell cars and your local municipality is installing a new public transport service, then that is probably a competitor. If you have none, then you probably need to take a long hard look and ask why has no one done this or why is there no-one else interested in this market?

Don't get me wrong, if you have an amazing business idea like building a rocket to get to Mars, then your competitors may be hard to find, but they're there.

Competitors are very valuable because they're the ones we can best model. Not copy, but model.
If you're just starting out or implementing new systems then now is not the time to reinvent the wheel. Improve on it not rebuild it. I

understand the need to be different and unique, but there is a time and a place for that. If you have lots of funds backing you then by all means go ahead and do it but while you are starting out, do what works with a few tweaks here and there. Don't recreate a new wheel just yet.

So let's get into it.

Doing a competitive analysis will give you an idea of what the market is willing to pay for items and what is currently working. You get to see it without committing all your money behind the unknown.

What I need you to do is look at your competitors and answer the following. Again this may not be too obvious.

I helped a real estate business in an area with an unusually high proportion of retirees. We asked a few questions and found out that a lot of property decisions were being put on the back-burner because of an abundance of cheap cruises available. This is not a competitor that I would ever have spotted without asking.

Your Competitors

Who are they.......

What are they offering.......

Your Competitors

> # What added value are they offering.......

> # What is their price point.......

Now that we got started on researching competitors we get to do something fun with that information. Remember: do not be selective with the information you gather. Look at a minimum of ten competitors. The more the better. I would cap it at around twenty.

It is time to do a SWOT analysis of your competitors. What are their Strengths, Weakness, what Opportunities do you see that they overlooked, and what potential Threat are they to your business.

The reason we are doing this, is so that you can learn from what works for them and what does not. By looking at your competitors, you take out all the guesswork on what your market wants, and you can hit the ground running.

At the end of the day it is about working smarter not harder.

Remember you are not going to copy what they do, you are using it as a starting point when working on your business. Model what works, never copy – it's not cool, people are not stupid and copyright issues are a nightmare that just make lawyers rich.

All you are doing now is getting a clear direction of what the market wants and expects. It also means you know how much you can push the boundaries.

This is not about undercutting anyone.

That is the biggest no-no in business, never be in a price race to zero.

All that will end up doing is driving you out of business before you even start. Charge a reasonable market rate and if you can charge slightly more, but give value for that price. Have your clients know and understand that they got value from doing business with you instead of your competitors.

5 BRANDING

The image they see.

The perception they have.

It does not matter if you are a service or product based business, you need to have a brand identity. More than that, you need to have a cohesive brand.

A brand helps your customers understand and know who you are. It is not enough to just give your business a name these days. Your business needs to stand for something.

Right now if I had to walk up to a women and say Tiffany's - one of two things will come to mind. Breakfast at Tiffany's and the little blue box. That little blue box is exactly what I mean by branding. It is association, it is giving your customers a distinct look and feel for your business and without even looking at the name, just by the look of something they will know it is yours.

It's important to not get bogged down in too much technical detail. Don't worry about how that vision will be realised or executed. If you have a good idea of what you want your branding to look like and can convey this to someone else, then you're on track. There are several very good websites where you can employ a design professional to bring your vision to life, just spend a few dollars and get it done. There's no need to learn Photoshop just to hack out a few designs, and unless you have tons of experience, a professional will probably do a better job. This is a common mistake we all make, we try to be everything and do everything in our businesses, and sometimes this is just not the most sensible route to take. You have to look at the bigger picture and not sweat the small stuff.

To help you along and get the branding portion out of the way, follow the following guidelines. Remember this is not meant to be overly completed. I am giving you these guidelines so that you can easily convey what you want to someone else. This will give them a good starting point and get their creative juices flowing. If you are the creative type then go for it yourself.

1. <u>Who are you? - Things that describe your brand</u>

> The physical product is important, but only secondary to the emotions that your branding needs to convey. There's a difference between "we clean carpets in rentals" to "We provide a trusted cleaning service to landlords, who rely on our integrity to get the job done at the scheduled time with complete confidence that everything in the home will be treated with respect and will be completely secure."

_____

_____

_____

2. **<u>Colour and fonts - Colour can trigger emotion</u>**

Colour is vital to a brand, and nothing resonates as well psychologically as colour. Imagine Cadbury's Purple or Coca-Cola Red. The tone and intensity of your colour choices dominate all other branding and go a long way to determining your corporate culture and the way the public see you. If you're not sure of your colour choices then it's well worth the investment to consult a good design consultancy. Get this right.

_____

_____

_____

3.   **<u>Logo - If you already have one - or need one</u>**

Logos are important, but they're replaceable and interchangeable. Every serious business needs a good logo, but finding this logo can be a process, and the logo will change and adapt over time. If you've determined your corporate identity and colours then relay this information to a few designers on Fiverr or something similar and see what they come up with. You'll probably find that $20 spent will result in a perfectly useful logo.

Draw a basic concept here, or just leave it to a designer.

4. Feeling - What feeling does your brand convey?

This is where congruence comes in. To portray a feeling or emotion, you need to use the same branding throughout your presentation and across media. Think of a large insurance company that needs to instil trust, what paper do they use, what fonts, what colours. What they say becomes less relevant because the presentation has already built that feeling of trust, so they at no point need to say "you can trust us", it's assumed.

_____

_____

_____

_____

While we tackle branding , we need to look at your brand story and your 'about' page.

If you don't yet have an 'about' page then that's okay, we can fix that now. Your 'about' page is crucial because besides your homepage that is usually the second most visited page on websites. A website is not crucial but most of us have one and why have something you are not going to monetise on. At the end of the day if it is not bringing in traffic or sales then it is just costing you.

The 'about' page is overlooked by so many companies and it is really sad, this is a chance to have a vital call to action. A statement that tells them what to do next. After all, you have just told a client all about you and then, while they are primed and ready, you need to strike and convert them.

Writing an 'about' page can be a bit daunting and overwhelming. That is why I have broken it down for you, so that you can have an 'about' page on your sight in a few minutes.

So to write a good about page you need to cover a few things. This is about telling clients who you are, where you have come from, the roadblocks along the way that brought you to this current business.

1. <u>**Your Backstory - Why Should I Take Notice**</u>

Give the backstory to this product/business/opportunity.

How did it start?

What was the inspiration?

What caused you to decide to build this?

2. <u>**Your Desires**</u>

Here you want to look for an emotional trigger, something that gets your potential customer to go "me too" "yes, I understand".

This is usually an external desire, something that people can easily aspire to and imagine for themselves.

3.   The Wall You Hit

Every good story has a conflict, a point-of-no-return, a decision beyond which everything changes. You need to find this because this is where you emotionally bond with the reader. If you're able to get them to imagine themselves in a similar situation then they immediately have a personal interest in the outcome.

4.   The New Opportunity or Business You Discovered (how or why you started this business)

This is your opportunity to paint your offer as a mission, as more than just a means to extract money from your clients. For example "We needed to find a way to redefine the automotive service industry, because it is after all about service first, and not just fixing cars."

5. The Plan

This is your grand plan, and if the reader is by now emotionally invested in your story, then they have internalised and personalised the wall and the opportunity, and they are ready to accept your solution.

This needs to be a change from their current situation, and not just an improvement. The psychological process is different and a complete change, a different way of doing things. This is much easier for most people to accept.

A change implies that they're doing things wrong at the moment, which brings on feelings of personal responsibility, and no-one wants to admit that they made a mistake or did wrong. A complete change indicates that the responsibility is external, the system is broken, it's someone else's fault.

6.   The Result

This is the confusing part. The result doesn't need to be the end of your story, or even any type of success at all. On a physical level it could just honestly be the position at which you currently are: "Our first workshop will open in a week, and we couldn't be more excited because ..."

The important part is that you show an emotional transformation, some reason for the reader to attach to you on an emotional level, and you'll have a committed follower.

This is where they get to know, like and trust you as an individual or brand.

Now it's your turn to try your hand at writing an 'about' page. Remember to include a call to action at the end or you would have just wasted your time. I would suggest having your call to action linked to a sales funnel . It honestly is a game changer.

Remember, also, that your 'about' page does not have to be a long elaborate university style essay, just take each heading we have given you and write a few lines. It really is that easy – just be honest and genuine about what it is you are offering your clients.

If you want, your 'about' section could even be a video of you explaining who you are and why you are doing what you are doing. This way clients get a true feel of who you are.

6 CLIENT STORY

It is not about you, it is about them.

Yes, it **is** about them.

One of the most common mistakes business owners make is thinking about themselves and not their clients. You are important, but not when it comes to your business. You need to learn to separate yourself from your business. Yes it's your business but you cannot take it personally. In business your client is king. This is because, at the end of the day, you are not the one buying your services or product - they are.

So why would you set up something that appeals to yourself and not them. This business is to serve your clients and not yourself. Give your client what they want and never hold back. We mean that when we say it, do not hold back. Always give your customers value and never have them feeling like they've been short changed or getting the bare minimum. Over-deliver in every instance. They must feel that the experience they got from you, whether in person or on a site, was worth more than the money they paid.

Now in order to give your clients what they want you need to know who your client actually is. Who is your product or service for?

Up to now we have discussed what business you are in, what your competitors are doing and what your brand is. Now comes the exciting bit. Putting it all together and getting a better picture of who your client is and what they want.

To help you understand what your client may want from you, here is some questions to help you answer that.

1. **What problems does your client have?**

This is usually an obvious, physical need. For example a physical need to lose weight.

2. **What limiting beliefs do your customer have around purchasing your product?**

These usually relate to negative associations related to similar products or services. For example "I've tried Atkins and Paleo and Ketones, and I just can't stick to it. I suffer through it for a while and then always cheat. I'm not strong enough. Diets don't work for me."

3. **What problem does your service or product solve?**

Here we delve a little deeper. This is not the same as your physical product, this is about the emotion or underlying need that is being fulfilled. Most gym memberships are not about physical fitness, but about community and friendships. Most fuel stations sell convenience, not gas and diesel.

This is where the concept of an alternative instead of an improvement comes in. Your product needs to be a green-field alternative (come over to the other side where the grass is greener) not an improvement that makes them feel bad about failing with previous attempts. If you understand the underlying emotion then it's easier to frame your offering in such a way that it speaks directly to that need as a new option and not just an improvement.

4.   **What problems will your solution cause?**

Every solution causes a new set of problems and a new set of opportunities. A change in diet to raw vegetables may, for example, cause confusion as to what and how to prepare meals, which leads to a new opportunity to offer daily menu suggestions or a done-for-you delivered service. This list can be pretty large, and it keeps changing, so it's vital to get constant feedback from your customers.

This is a lot to think about, but trust me, if you can relate to your client and speak to their problems and pains you will see the results. This is because you will be giving them what they want and presented in a way that is a no brainer for them to take up the offer.

Now that you have a better understanding of your clients' problems and how you can provide them with a solution, we can start building a better understanding of your client.

You need to understand that at the end of the day your client is more than just dollar signs , they are people just like you and me and the more human emotion and care we can put into our business the more profit you will see. Not only that, you will slowly start building up a following of loyal customers who want whatever you are doing or selling because they believe in your message and product.

So now back to your client, what I find the most useful when looking at any business is to build an avatar by building a story or a persona for your ideal client. You see when you can build a mental image of your client you are able to better serve them. Anyone can say "oh my clients are a young families with just one kid". But what does that actually look like and mean.

It would be more beneficial for you to say. "My clients are first time parents who have just purchased a home and have a well-established career. Before starting a family they enjoyed going to local events and enjoyed trying out different cultural cuisines.".

Do you see what we are doing here, by building a profile? We are building up a story that you can refer to, and in a way get in these clients heads and know what would be appealing to them. From this story can now see that these ideal clients are going to be open to things that talk about their new child, open to new ideas and experimenting. They are also very driven as they have a well established career and are financially secure, so they can afford to pay for what we're selling.

Is that not more useful than just saying my clients are first time parents. When you build a story or a persona you get to see who they are and what they want. It also gives you a chance to see if this is the type of clients you want to work with, especially in a service based industry.

So I urge you to create your client persona now and see who your ideal client is.

7 LEAD MAGNETS

What is a Lead Magnet

Do I even need it?

Let us start at the simplest answer: Yes, you need lead magnets.

A lead magnet is, in essence, your invitation. It is an item you give away for free to start a relationship. In the good old days this would be the beautiful flower presented to a lady – given without reservation or expectation, but with hope and love.

This can be a pdf guide to recipes if, for example, you sell weight loss items. Or it can be a book you send where the customer just pays shipping. You've probably seen the offers before: "Get my recipe book free, all you have to do is cover shipping" This then creates a lead who has given you their name, email, and physical address.

So in essence a lead magnet is an item or object that attracts your potential clients (leads). Like an invitation you give someone to a party or event, the invite is what intrigues them and has them wanting to know more. A lead magnet is what you use to get your foot in the door.

So let's look more at what Lead Magnets are with a few examples:

They are things like, mini training session, how-to guides, look books, printables, webinars, books, product etc. The key thing to lead magnets is that it is something you give clients for free or almost free in exchange for their contact details. The almost free involves things like books or sample products, where you give the product for free and they just pay shipping. What we'll also sometimes do is charge $1 for a lead magnet because people tend to respect something that they've paid for much more than a free item.

Your ideal clients will give you their email address in exchange for your lead magnet because you understand who your client is and what appeals to them. You have just looked at a client persona and now you can use that to create a lead magnet to introduce them to your service or product.

Your lead magnet also gives your ideal clients an obligation-free way to test the waters, to see if you are who they want to do business with. Once they give you their email address you can nurture that relationship, and build to a sale.

Your lead magnets should be designed to solve your clients' problem, and focus on their issues. Remember in Chapter 6 where I had you look at what problems your clients had. Well, your lead magnet should speak to that problem and what they need or could use to solve that problem.

My advice is create a few lead magnets and test which ones your clients actually want. What you will start seeing is that some lead magnets will speak more to your clients' needs and problems, and these are the good ones to use and expand on.

Here are some tips to creating a good lead magnet:

1. Content must always relate to your markets' pain points

2. Be of value and be able to get them results

3. Simple and easy to read 300-500 words unless it is a book

Once you have created a few lead magnets you are going to need to give them away, and there is no better place to give things away than on social media.

First you'll need a headline, something to capture your audience's attention, remember if you are marketing on social media then you need to stop them from scrolling and get them actually looking at your content. So a good headline is key. It will grab them and get them hooked on what you have to say.

I have some examples to show you but first here are a few things to think about when doing your own headlines.

1. Negative and slightly controversial headlines convert better

2. Capitalize The First Character Of Every Word In Your Headline

3. Speak to their pain points- things they worry about

4. Balance headlines, 3 negative and 2 positive

I know it is easy said than done, so to help you along I have 5 headlines you can use to get you going and thinking of your own. In the examples you need to fill in the blanks with how it relates to your lead magnet you just created. I have included an example for the health industry.

Examples:

1. 3 Tricks To….. (healthy skin)

2. What Everybody Ought To Know About……. (the keto diet)

3. Your ……(personal trainer) Doesn't Want You To Read This Because ……(you don't need them)

4. Little Known Ways To…. (lose weight while sleeping)

5. Tired Of…….(having no energy)

Hopefully that gives you more of an idea of an attention grabbing headline that gets your client to do a double take and read your content. As I said earlier I am not holding back anything, so I will tell you what I do to create headlines. I use a program to do it. If you are good at copywriting and content creation then skip this part and stop reading and go to the next chapter, however if you are like me and can maybe come up with one or two headlines and emails and that is about it then you need help. For years Shawn and I struggled coming up with what to write in our automation emails and it was feeling so fake and forced and the headlines - let's not even go there, it was bad. It was a sheer miracle that we even had an acceptable open rate.

Honestly I figured "you know what, I need to admit" when I have reached something beyond my pay-grade. I searched around and found someone to write copy for me, but thing is - it cost me just over a thousand dollars each time. I don't know about you but I could not see myself forking out that amount of money for each copywriting project I had. So I searched around and found cheaper options on virtual assistance type sites but I wanted faster and more reliable. Remember we are all about smarter not harder.

That is where I stumbled across Funnel Scripts , it is like a 100 copywriters all in one software. To give you a brief idea it does ad , sales, call to action copies , email scripts, headlines, email subject lines and as you know my subject lines on emails left a lot to be desired so for just that alone I was doing a happy dance. It also has lead capture scripts and lots more.

It really is so simple all you have to do is go to a template, answer a few questions and a second later out pops your headlines and all the copy things you need. Wait for it, it even gives you more than 5 headline options to choose from, so you can choose whichever one you feel would be the best first or split test it.

Now don't get me wrong this is not for everyone, but honestly if you want one less headache in your business and want to focus on selling, then let that side of things be taken care of. If you have an assistant you can even get them to fill out the template and boom just like that you have freed up even more of your time. That is what I did anyway.

Funnel Scripts has helped me and it is only right that I share this information with you. This will help you get an idea of what your market wants and it also means you get to narrow in on your brand message and what sense you want clients to have when they come across your content.

Another good way to also get an idea is to look at what others in a similar market are doing, but not your direct competitors. The reason

I say not your direct competitors is because you do not want to end up stealing their content. If you look at a similar market you get an idea of what is possible and how you can adapt it to suit what you need.

8 CONTENT CREATION

Publishing is key.

The medium is irrelevant.

Consistency is vital.

When I talk about publishing I do not necessarily mean go out and write a book, however if you can, then go for it. What I am talking about is publishing content, getting your message and views across and consistently doing that.

The reason you need to be publishing is to get your audience and clients aware that you exist and have something to offer them, and also because long after you have published it, that information is still out there, still able to be viewed by your potential clients. It's like free advertising constantly coming in and creating leads for you.

It also has another effect - it gives you more credibility. You will stand out better than your competitor if you have, for example, 300+ podcast episodes or numerous blog posts giving clients tips and advice.

When it comes to publishing there is no "one size fits all" approach. I could tell you that right now videos are getting better traction that written words, but that may not be the case next month. The thought of having a camera in your face also petrifies most people and may not be for you. That is fine, you need to do what works for you and bests suits your personality and market. The key is consistency. You need to stick to it.

If you feel comfortable in front of a camera then video will be your best option because this can easily be repurposed, and in all honesty gives video the most value. Even if you never plan on publishing it, and just rip out the audio, I would still start with video any way. That material, no matter how bad, may become useful later.

If you're more comfortable writing long form posts or even blog articles, then do that, but block out the time, put some thought into it, and publish consistently. If you can't spare the time to post every day then commit to twice or three times a week, or even once a week.

If you're doing half hour videos then a daily schedule can be a bit hectic and it would probably be more realistic to commit to once a week. I will get more into scheduling in the next chapter. For now I want you to get comfortable with the idea of sharing your message.

It may feel weird at first, and that is fine. That is where you started and you know what, your customer wants to see that you are real and not all perfect. This just adds credibility and realism. We all had to start somewhere.

When you think about your content, it should be genuine and honest, no fake content please. Remember: at the end of the day you are communicating with people, not machines. You are communicating with your ideal client here. So make sure that what you are publishing is actually adding value for them and not just publishing for the sake of it. It's all about them.

Now the big question - what to publish and when. The standard, across most markets, is to produce three posts adding value, then one that is an indirect sale. What I mean by an indirect sale is that you are not coming out of the gate asking them to buy your product. You are giving them value and then saying oh by the way if you want yours you can get it here. Or something along the lines of "I have a new project opening up in a few days I cannot wait for you to join me." That is considered a call to action.

The reason we do it this way is to start building a relationship with your clients and because you have been giving so much value to your audience they are easier to sell to, as they are already a believer in what you do. They can trust in what you have said because you have spent so much time giving them value.

Now there is one more piece of content you have to do every 10 or so posts and that is something funny, something entertaining. It could be a funny picture a blooper reel or just something funny that has happened in your life. This brings back the focus to you being a person and also gives your brand a personality.

There are a few places you can add your content to and share your message. By no means is this a full list but just the current ones to date. You will notice that I do not talk about your business website in this list. And I will tell you why in a bit, for now I want you to focus on publicly available platforms that you can use.

Below are the current best ways that you can publish content to your market, they are in no particular order

1. Facebook- both lives and posting

2. Podcasts

3. Medium (more for blogging)

4. Instagram

5. YouTube

6. Pinterest

So as you can see all the above are big social media platforms and the reason we show you them first is because that is going to give you the best traction over the shortest amount of time to get your message out there. These social platforms already have loyal followings and subscribers so what you are doing is using that to your advantage.

These things constantly change, so if by the time you read this a new player has hit the social scene, use it.

Now, about your own website: If you are starting out in doing content then it is probably not a good idea to publish content on your site. The reason we do not advise you to use your own site first is because it's generally a waste of time. You do not have the traffic or clout that these social sites have, and marketing is about drawing traffic to your offer. Also, things like SEO and algorithms come into play and honestly it is a mind field when you are just starting out.

If you have a blog installed – Wordpress is great for this - then copy the content you place on social platforms on your own site, but do not use your site as the only or main means of getting your message across. No one will see it at first.

So have a think about what you are comfortable with and start writing that content and sharing your message.

9 LEVERAGE YOUR CONTENT

Make the most of your words.

Working smarter not harder.

After going through the effort of creating all this content, you need to make it work for you. And this is all about working smarter and not harder.

First, having the content on its own is amazing and will get you results and engagement. Having consistent content already puts you ahead of the game and gives you an edge. Now it is time to kick it up a notch and start leveraging those words. It is all about getting the most mileage out of your content.

So what I am going to share with you is how we leverage our content on the social media platforms we have.

First order of business, we do not have just one platform that we use. We are omni-present. Which means we are on a lot of platforms sharing our message and content.

Remember I have three children which means time is valuable and I need to make the time I have count.

The reasons we made the business decision to use more than one publishing platform is so that not all our eggs are in one basket. What happens when Facebook closes down your page for whatever reason, or Youtube decides to shadow-ban you because of an alleged copyright strike? You will be completely stuck if that was your only platform.

It is fine to start out with one platform, but make provision in your plan to grow your social presence. Also, it is no more effort to be on other platforms as well, since there are many software programs that will allow you to preschedule your posts. So you can set and forget.

One notable exception is doing 'lives' - try and not schedule them. I know there are programs out there that will allow you to do that and it is easy to do, but try use them to a minimum, or mix it up so that your audience cannot tell that it is recorded. The reason I say this is because a lot of the time people jump on to live session in the hope you will mention their name and acknowledge them. When you pre-rerecorded the live, you lose that option you lose that connection that people expect from 'lives'. So some magic can be lost.

Now onto how our businesses leverage content. I am going to give a simple version of it and then we are going to dissect it and get into more detail.

As you can see in the simple content leverage stream. You are taking a piece of content and sharing it on four different platforms. As you can see it is not that hard to put yourself on more than one platform. In the simple leverage stream the hardest part is actually coming up with the content that needs to be shared. The rest just takes a few minutes of your time to get done each day.

Content Stream

Simple Leverage

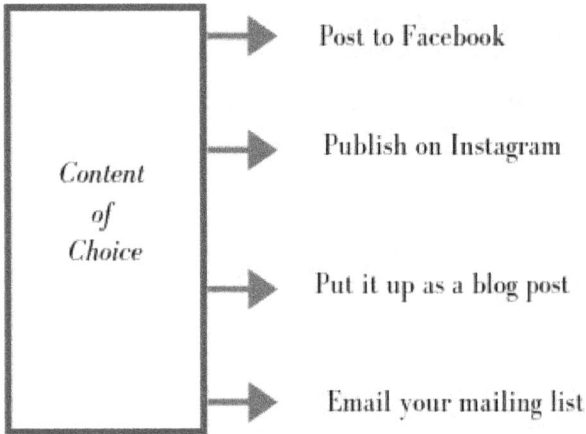

Content of Choice	→ Post to Facebook
	→ Publish on Instagram
	→ Put it up as a blog post
	→ Email your mailing list

So if you are getting started in business I would suggest doing the simple stream to start off with and then move on to the slightly more complicated one I am about to share. If however you have a team or an assistant them jump straight to the bigger leverage stream.

The best way to leverage your content is to follow what I am about to tell you, it does take some time but what it will end up doing is give you content over a period of 90 days, which means once you have created the content you do not have to look at it again for a few weeks (aside from 'lives'). Which, let's be honest, is the best way to leverage not only your content but your time as well, because now you do not have to worry every few days on what information you are going to put up or share with your audience.

So let's jump into how this all works and flows.

Step 1: Research

It may take you a few days to do this but it is worth it. Want to do is research 90 to 100 topics you can talk about or discuss with your audience. The key in researching this is looking at questions your audience is currently asking and this way you can provide the answers to them. You can use tools like Google trends, BuzzSumo, Social Mention to help in your research. Read competitor's blogs, forums, Q&A sites, review sites, anywhere where your clients may be asking questions or for advice.

Step 2: Content

Now comes the fun bit, creating the content. You already have what you are going to talk about from the research you have done, it is now just about adding your spin or keys points to it. Basically fleshing it out each question or sub-question to a topic that is about 500 -1000 words long.

Step 3: Creation

Let's create it, what you are going to do is record a video for each one of your topics you just created. So you should end up with around 90 to 100 videos ranging between 3-10minutes long. Do not worry if you do not want to be on camera, you can use the audio with just a static image or a collection of slides. The recording just needs to be in a video format.

Also, the video quality is not too relevant. Almost any smartphone will be perfect. People will forgive almost anything on video, you could be outside, birds could be swooping around you, it does not matter at all.

Audio is a completely different matter. If they battle to hear what you say then expect every second comment to be about that. Happily that is extremely easy to solve, and there is a massive range of lavalier and interview microphones that are inexpensive and work perfectly with your phone – get one.

Now the following steps are what I would suggest you hand over to someone else and not do yourself. You can do it yourself but, at the end of the day, we want to leverage your time and your content, and if you are doing it yourself then you are not gaining much more time in your day.

Step 4: Video Narrative

Unless you read the content you created word for word (which I do not suggest because it almost always ends up sounding robotic) then there will be some difference between what you created and what you said. There are several services where a person extracts the text, but they are more expensive, so what you probably want to do is use a service such as Temi to transcribe your video. Just do a quick quality check through each video to confirm that there's no mistakes.

Step 5: Podcast

Rip the audio down from your video so that it can be used as an episode on your podcast.

Step 6: Publish

Publish your video on YouTube and release a notice on all your social media accounts that you have a video up. The same happens for your podcast.

Step 7: Blog Post

Take the content that you created for the video and have it SEO optimised to be placed on Medium, and if you have one, your own blog site.

Step 8: Social Posts

Create long form posts, this is like a highlight version of the bigger post. No more than 300 words. These can be used to place on social media.

Step 9: Quote Cards

Extract keys phrases from your content and create 3-4 quote cards from each post, little inspirations which get your audience thinking and re-engaged.

Step 10: Social Graphics

Use content (mostly just stills) from the videos to create graphics that can be used on all your social platforms, as images to go with your posts. Remember each social platform has their own graphic requirements.

Step 11: Video Clips

Create a 60 to 90 second highlight clip of each video to be used on Facebook and Instagram. Again each have their own requirements and these do change occasionally.

This may seem like a lot of steps and things to do but it is definitely worth it. What I suggest is that you start small and grow from there. I would suggest outsourcing from step 4 on words, because these steps have to do with a lot of editing and slog work. Your focus should be on your business and growing it, not getting the fonts correct on a graphic.

A tip in following this sequence is recording 5-10 videos at the same time. That way you can knock out a lot of content in a short space of time. It also means you can spread the whole job out over a few days. It not only gives you a chance to recharge and not feel drained, but if you are doing videos and not just still, it means you give yourself time to do outfit changes.

Outfit changes are key, so that it does not look like the video was shot at the same time, so change up the scenery as well. It gives more authenticity and believability to the content.

Now you can see that by having this much content out there you will have increased your engagement with your audience on whatever platform works for them. And have a greater chance of making your presence known.

So now we need to figure out when and how to publish all this content. Following is one way you can distribute your content. This is just one way, do what works best for you and your business.

Content Stream

Podcast

Post daily on it and use the first video you created
and follow the correct sequence

Youtube

Post daily in the same sequence as the Podcast but
be 1-2 days behind. Remember to include a link
back to the Podcast

Facebook

Post daily and use a randomised collection of the
highlight clips created, social posts and quote cards

Instagram

Post daily and use a randomised collection of the highlight clips created, social posts and quote cards

Blog

Post daily and use a randomised collection of the highlight clips created, social posts and quote cards

Other Social Platforms

Post daily and use a randomised collection of the highlight clips created, social posts and quote cards

So there you have it, how we leverage our content. It does take some time to set up and get the ball rolling but once you do it you will have content ready to go, and free you up to do other things. There are also programs and assistance you can use to upload and post the content for you. Remember to keep track of where you post what so that you do not post the same thing twice in one week.

It is OK to re-use or repeat content. Most social media has a memory of less than 2 weeks, so if a single post or quote card is repeated after a few weeks there is a very good chance that no-one will ever notice. If you repeat too often then it will be noticed and the account will quickly go stale and start losing engagement.

10 CLIENT JOURNEY

Website traffic.

Where do they go?

Everyone has a website these days and having just a website is not good enough. Yes I have a website, but I do not depend on it to bring in my sales, for that I use a sales funnels as it covers everything, but more about that later. For now we need to focus on how traffic works and what that means for your business.

Whether you are using a traditional website to sell your service or product or a sales funnel you would use the same traffic method as anyone else. So by traffic we mean sending customers to your offer. You can do this several different ways, by running ads on social platforms, doing banner ads on other people's blogs, running a shout out campaign, doing giveaways. The list goes on. But essentially the goal from any one of these avenues is to drive traffic back to your site or sales page.

What a lot of new business owners do not understand is that more traffic does not necessarily relate to more sales. When we run any of the above mentioned traffic options it is considered cold traffic. The reasons it is cold traffic is because these people that see your ad have probably never heard of you or don't even know that you exist, so it will take a lot longer for them to learn to know, like, and eventually trust you.

These type of leads need at least 4 to 7 touch points in order to make a purchase from you. Meaning they will need to see your ad, website or communication from you more than four times before they take any action, depending on the price point of your product or service it can take up to an average of seven touch points for a lead to hand over their money.

This is because only when they first see your ad, or message do they become aware of who you are and what you offer. Once they see more information or all of the content you provide they get to know , like and trust what you have to offer . Giving you credibility. This is all about building a relationship in a short space of time.

Do not freak out about that, it is normal to have that many touch points with a lead or prospective client and is part of running a business.

So now, in order to build the relationship quicker and not wait for them to come back to your site or your social platform to see your content. We need to do an extra step that most of the time gets overlooked by competitors.

Retargeting is like the magic button that allows those touch points to happen without you having to physically put in the hard work. So ensure you have your Facebook pixel and Google tracking installed (this is what allows retargeting). Even if you do not intend to use retargeting immediately, the tracking is vital because when you need it, it will be good to have more profiling data, so set up tracking now. I am not going into how to do these as they change frequently, but ample how-to guides are available online.

This is what those annoying ads that follow you use. Have you ever clicked on something and then changed your mind and all of a sudden it's on everything you look at. That is retargeting in action, I love it in business but I hate it when I am trying to do some retail therapy.

What a lot of business owners do not realise is that once a client hits your website for the first time, most leave almost immediately. This is normal. The ones who stay do not instantly convert and they go on what I call the Client Journey. This journey is most common on traditional websites that do not use things like sales funnels or landing pages.

To make it easier for you to understand the Client Journey and what it would look like if a client had to stumble on your site or ad and the journey they would follow, we have included the graphic below.

It shows that a customer can go through various stages when looking at your content, ranging from awareness to loyalty. The key here is to just understand that the more content and information you put out the more your potential client is able to make a decision on whether to work with you or not.

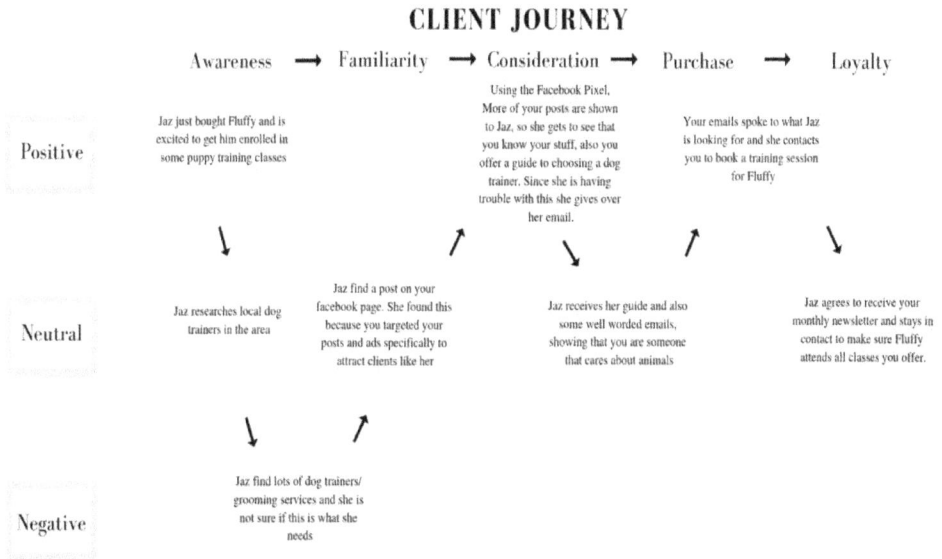

CLIENT JOURNEY

Awareness → Familiarity → Consideration → Purchase → Loyalty

Positive

Jaz just bought Fluffy and is excited to get him enrolled in some puppy training classes

Using the Facebook Pixel, More of your posts are shown to Jaz, so she gets to see that you know your stuff, also you offer a guide to choosing a dog trainer. Since she is having trouble with this she gives over her email.

Your emails spoke to what Jaz is looking for and she contacts you to book a training session for Fluffy

Neutral

Jaz researches local dog trainers in the area

Jaz find a post on your facebook page. She found this because you targeted your posts and ads specifically to attract clients like her

Jaz receives her guide and also some well worded emails, showing that you are someone that cares about animals

Jaz agrees to receive your monthly newsletter and stays in contact to make sure Fluffy attends all classes you offer.

Negative

Jaz find lots of dog trainers/ grooming services and she is not sure if this is what she needs

The aim of the content you have created and the information you have on your website is to get them moving from having a basic awareness about you to making a purchase and being loyal to your business or brand.

If you are using just a website then you need to pay close attention to where your audience is going on your site. There are several plugins and extensions you can add to your website that will enable you to get real time information and track their actions.

I know it may sound a bit creepy to follow someone on your site but believe me, it will pay off in the end. It will close off loopholes and will also help you better understand which areas may need more work and attention.

I remember when I first launched my photography studio and I had the first website up and running. I would spend hours at the computer watching if anyone came in and where they went. What I learnt was that the gallery was almost always the first port of call and not the information on what type of sessions I offered. I then moved the gallery to the front page to make it easy for clients to get the information they needed and not go and search for it.

I was making their life easier and as such it became easier for them to say yes to the booking with me.

The aim at the end of the day is to make it easier for your potential clients to get to say yes to working or buying from you. Also we want to remove any objections or difficulties they may be having about committing to a sale.

11 BUILD A TEAM

If you want to grow,

Build a team.

In order for your business to grow, and it not be just you stuck in another job under the banner of being self-employed, you need to grow. And you need to grow quickly. I do not want you buying a job for yourself.

The reason I stress growing quickly and building a team is because you do not want to get comfortable doing everything. That is a recipe for disaster. It will quickly lead you to a point where the business does not have enough power and momentum to grow beyond yourself.

I had this vision of being my own boss not letting anyone tell me when I can have lunch and when I can have a cup of coffee. Having to schedule with someone else when I would be allowed to just take a few minutes to eat or, even worse, being forced to eat when I was not ready. At work I was a star employee, at work early, always giving above and beyond and helping out wherever I could, but inside I was dying. The sheer will that it took to get out of bed each morning, to wash rinse and repeat, each day was doing my head in.

I knew I needed to change the situation.

That is when I decided to become my own boss, play by my own rules and say goodbye to the 7am starts and do my own thing. What a wakeup call that decision was to me. I was now the receptionist, the boss, the accountant, the social media person, the product creator. I was it all. Anything that needed to happen in the business needed to be done by me. Depression was taking hold of my mind and now I felt I was worse off than before, my hours were longer, still being awake at 2 am so that orders went out the next day with the first courier. It felt like I was in a living hell.

As I sat drinking my cold coffee which at some point was warm and dry toast (my brain was that occupied that I forgot to even butter it) it hit me, why am I doing it alone? What am I trying to prove to myself? How is this business ever going to get anywhere or grow if all my time is being taken up with trying to just do every little task in it.

I started putting the feelers out and building a team, a support network to keep me sane. This is where I learnt that if I want to have a business and grow it, I needed to build a team and delegate.

I am not the best at social media so that is why I get someone else to do that. Copywriting is not my thing and, as you know, now I have a software that does it for me. I am now in the position where I can be creative and help other business owners improve their business and I know that while I am doing that everything in the background is running and functioning mostly without me.

This is the magic of having a team. Now don't worry, you do not have to go and hire a whole lot of people and have them in the office with you. I can understand that the thought of getting all the paperwork and having to deal with things like payroll can be another headache in itself. What you can use to get going is a virtual assistant or even contract agencies to look after certain aspects you need help with. The main thing for you to do is focus on WHO can do the work for you not HOW they are going to do it.

Your job is to stick to what you are good at and let your team handle the rest. This way you are always playing to your strengths and will have a more successful business.

Having a business is not about working yourself to death, it is about serving your clients by helping them solve a problem. So I encourage you to build your team and focus on what you are good at.

The one thing you will learn in your business journey is that money is faster than time. Use your money to get the right people around you so that your time is better spent.

Your business plan will dictate which tasks are repetitive and which are once-off. Generally things like logo design are an irregular task, and can be contracted on a per-assignment basis on sites like Fiverr or Upwork. If you need regular work done like data processing, then the best would be to employ a VA or remote worker on a weekly or monthly basis. Either way, you should have a better idea than most of what jobs can be outsourced. It's hard to decide what to trust someone else to do, but this needs to be done.

Much more important than hiring is firing, and this we learned from Gary Vaynerchuk. If it's not working out then terminate the relationship and move on. Be reasonable, but be decisive. Hiring is unknown and depends on faith. Firing is an absolute obligation to your business based on fact and experience. If someone is not performing to expectation then they are just costing you money, and it's time to cut the cord.

When you start looking at employng a team in the office with you, do not go out and hire the first person that ticks all the options on the checklist, make sure they have a personality that you feel you can work with. Have fun with it and remember if you are hiring then that means that you have reached a milestone in your business, so enjoy the process.

12 SALES FUNNELS

Funnels are game changers,

Time to change it up.

I came from the generation that remembers when Gmail first launched and wanting to be one of the first to get a Gmail account. And yes my Gmail account is that old. It was a time when websites where these big impressive things that you had to have a sitemap just to navigate them.

So the logical thing to do when we started any business was to get a domain name and get a website. The designing and set up of the website is not something that happens overnight, especially when things like SEO and hidden pixels come into play. The last website we did took us well over a month to design and finalise.

Setting up websites are the ultimate brain drain of my creativity. Time and time again when it came to the website component of a new business venture I would stall till the very last moment because I knew I was in for endless nights of headaches trying to get things right.

At the end of the day all I wanted was a nice site that looked amazing and converted. Sadly unless I was running an e-commerce site my websites did not convert. I was frustrated to say the least. I installed a tracker on one of my sites and I could do a real time tracking of where on the site a person was, and even had the ability to pop up a message to them to try and engage with my audience.

The frustration now was that I could see people on my site and see them looking around but that was it, no one was going to the contact page to fill in their details.

Shawn and I sat down and figured there has to be a better way, because you can't tell me all the websites out there are doing nothing, we must be missing a step here. It honestly felt like we were leaving money on the table by not having this site convert at a much higher rate. We did some research and come across ClickFunnels. Now Russel Brunson and ClickFunnels showed us the missing link, the step we were missing in our website.

It was as if someone has just shown us where the light switch in the room was, we went from having a site that was used as basically a portfolio to now having something that was bringing in leads and all it took was one thing, one shift and things changed.

Funnels are game changers and if you are reading this book, it was probably a funnel that brought you here.

So now you are probably wondering what we did to get the site to bring in leads. Let me show you. We did several incremental steps, so let's start at the first thing we did.

We took our existing website and did not change it at all, what we needed was to first direct traffic to a landing page, so for the photography studio it was a free guide on how to look good when taking pictures. Who does not want to look good when taking pictures. It was such a brilliant lead magnet because it played to what people where already doing with "selfies" and now we were giving them a guide on how to make it look even better.

So because we had a landing page in front of our main website, it meant we were about to do something brilliant, we could grab emails addresses from the start. Now we did not have to wait for them to find the contact page, we were getting those emails upfront.

Because let's be honest pop ups get closed and ignored these days, so now we can grab an email address and then send out the guide while they have a look at the site and get a feel for the studio.

Now as we were learning about ClickFunnels we learnt all about sales funnels and how you can use ClickFunnels to build a sales page that converts and takes a lot of the stress off. So let me show you the example for the studio.

Using a sales funnel now means that I did not have to worry about my website as such, it became a place that if someone stumbled on it I would still be capturing their email but I could also then get them into the below funnel and convert them.

Example Studio Funnel

Landing Page Captures Email	Offer to book a chat to discuss needs	One time studio offer eg: Session fee only $29 not $100

In the example above the visitor is sent to a landing page where they are presented with just one offer – not at all confusing. In this case it was to enter their email address to download a free guide on how to take better selfies and pictures. After this they are sent to a bookings page offering a free chat to discuss their needs and give advice on how to get the best outcome from a photo session. They are then sent to a One-Time Offer page where they can get a heavily discounted session.

Now you can see that by using a sales funnel I was not just able to get an email address which I can later market to, I was also getting a proportion of the visitors to commit to a session with the studio. I will not get into all the details of what was on each page and what it looks like etc. What I am just showing you here and getting you to understand is what a sales funnel is.

A sales funnel is basically a way to convert on the spot and close the deal. Sales funnels basically replace the traditional website model of waiting for them to like everything they see and then possibly purchase. I think traditional websites are a relic of the early internet where people shopped online and then picked up the phone or visited your shop to make the purchase. Today they shop instore to physically test out and pick a product, and then buy online.

With a funnel you take them on a predesigned journey with a clear destination in mind. So like the example I shared, once someone says yes to the studio guide, and provides me with their email address, the system then sent them to a thank you page. On the thank you page they are asked if they want to book a free chat with me to discuss some session options we have, then they also get informed that because they got a guide they can get a one-time only session fee offer which is so good, it's a no-brainer to anyone considering a session, they would be a fool to say no.

I know you may be wondering about the cost of offering a free service or a massive discount. In the example above we took something that was getting no leads and converted it into something that was converting clients. If you are worried about the cost, do a self-liquidating offer where the income balances the cost and usually brings a small profit, then all leads are completely free. You don't need to use a loss leader to build a successful sales funnel.

13 ENTREPRENUER MATH

Numbers are fun.

Really.

This is a quick and easy chapter and not something that is meant to have you worried about numbers. To most people maths is a pain, but guess what, we all love counting the money.

Entrepreneur maths is easy though. Here goes:

If you get more out than you put in then it's profit.

I know this sounds too simple, but that's it. No complex financial calculations or projections. No income statements. All those things have their place, but right now we need simple.

Add up every part of a venture that will cost money in one list, then add up all the income streams that it generates in another list.

In - Out = Profit (unless it's negative, then it's a loss)

That's it. That's really all there is to it. Entrepreneur maths - so simple.

It's simple, but you need to do this. Know your expenses. Know your income. Know these numbers well, they're the lifeblood of your business.

This simple equation is then expanded on to give us more detail. Divide to get averages, multiply units to get totals. Easy stuff.

You need to know what it costs you to acquire a lead and what it brings back. There is no point spending $21 for on lead acquisition on a $19 sale. That is just bad math. Again, this is easy. Take the total ad spend on a campaign, eg. $210 and divide by the total number of sales from that campaign eg. 10

210/10 = 21   Cost per sale is $21

Total 10 sales @ $19each : 10x19 = $190

The only way you can justify the situation above is if you are marketing in your emails and making additional sales off that to offset the initial loss. This normally happens when you are intentionally running a "loss leader" campaign. For example a free book that they just cover the shipping but you can later sell more items to this customer because they are on your mailing list and you have a pre-defined sequence to sell them on other products..

The one place you really want to keep track of what you are spending and how it is tracking is when you run ads on social platforms. It is easy to overspend when you see lots of people commenting and engaging on your content. What you need to keep focus on is how much of that money is being converted into sales or else you are just bankrupting yourself.

There really is a lot of complexity, and if understanding financials where fun to you then you would have already taken the time to learn it. The rest of us need to understand what is profitable so can grow on that. The rest does not really matter much and is for the bookkeepers and accountants to figure out.

If your maths says that the business is constantly running a loss then it is a hobby and not a business. At that point you can rationally decide to keep it as it is or put it in the effort, make the changes needed, and turn it into a business.

14 CELEBRATIONS

Time to have fun.

Enjoy the moment.

I can remember as if it was yesterday, the first time Shawn and I sat down and plotted out what we wanted to achieve. How many sales we needed to be financially stable, and at the time it was like two or three sales, so we are not talking big numbers here people, but it meant actually sitting down and working out those costs. I remember thinking that if we have a thousand dollars a week we would be okay, we would not be doing cartwheels and living it up , but the bills would be paid and then we would be okay.

Looking back at it now, I don't know if I want to laugh or cry at myself because I remember thinking at the time how big a thousand dollar was, it may as well have been a million dollars a week. It felt like such an insurmountable figure and that was all that I could think about.

I started each day looking at this number on my closet door and it felt like such a slap in the face each morning when I did not make the target the day before, but being who I am , I just put a smile on and was all proud saying woohoo today is going to be awesome, but we all know I was filled with such dread inside. There is nothing as disheartening as a failed target.

I got to the point where I felt that we needed to take this note off the closet door immediately because it was just a constant reminder of my failure. That was when we both looked at this and figured out that we needed to flip the script for ourselves.

We started making a list of everything that happened in the business in that month. What were doing right on a daily business? If it was possible, you would have seen several light bulbs above my head because a switch was flipped. This was how celebration moments started for me.

Sitting there on the bed I realised that because I was so focussed on what I did not have, I had not noticed that the business was doing well. I had bookings a few months in advance, the bills were being paid and the money was coming in, just not in the way I had expected. I had a speaking engagement because of it and even had to interview a second photographer to ease the load.

You see what happened was that I forgot to celebrate the small moments in the business and instead I was just focussed on this one thing on my wall, which in my mind was basically a million dollars not a thousand - because that is what it felt like.

That was the moment when I realised that the key to staying sane in business and having the constant motivation to keep going when things feel like they are taking a few steps back, was to create celebration moments.

Using this one tool we have seen a positive change so many people's lives, when they too start to implement it. It is what takes you from a place of panic to one of joy, motivation and gratitude time and time again.

Okay so here is the deal. You need to get yourself a journal, diary or notebook. It cannot be something that is online. When you write something online you can't feel it, you can't embrace the emotion in the same way as you can in written form. Even in the digital world we are currently in there is still such a joy in opening a book and feeling the energy in it. Get a good old-fashioned book and a pen. Seriously. Do it.

This is the book that, each day, you use to write down your wins in business, and it does not have to be big things like a sale or landing a major contract. It can be as small as the fact that after three months you finally figured out how to get steam out of the coffee machine (true story).

I want you to take a few minutes at the end of each day and just jot down something good. If you say there was nothing good then I know you are lying and living in a place of fear and anxiety, because we all have one thing we can say was good today. It is okay if you start out small with, " the logo looked good on that Instagram post".

From there you take a few minutes at the end of the week and look through what you wrote and be present in the moment and celebrate it. Have a piece of cake, glass of bubbly, sparkling juice, whatever, but take this moment to celebrate all you have done this week. Look at each item, remember them and celebrate them.

This is honestly what has kept me motivated in business. We celebrate each week and in doing so we can see how far we have come. The children call the day between Thursday and Saturday Party-Friday because that's how they know it – there is a celebration every Friday.

Once you start learning to celebrate these moments, setting goals becomes easy. This is because you have seen how much you have been able to do in business, how far you have come, and how every big thing is just a process of small victories. This keeps you motivated.

It also means that when you get faced with big tasks like creating 90 pieces of video content and you achieve it you can look back and know that you managed to achieve something that at first may have seemed daunting but now is a breeze to create.

It is about building up a new set of beliefs, showing yourself that you have achieved success in business where you once saw failures.

ABOUT THE AUTHORS

Cindy and Shawn Pate make a unique combination and have thus been able to help business around the world find a fresh perspective and a new path to profitability. As a team, their diverse and unique ability are encouraged to shine and create a holistic picture of the business.

Shawn has decades of management and directorship experience and is able to see patterns and naturally gain a deeper understanding in the workings of a business.

Cindy is a spiritual consultant and able to naturally understand the human dynamics of an organization. Through this deeper understanding, she is able to assist owners and directions in releasing the blocks that hold them back and stifle the business. This is powerful.

www.ingramcontent.com/pod-product-compliance
Lightning Source LLC
Chambersburg PA
CBHW031946190326
41519CB00007B/686